Howard

Poetic Life

H.O.WARD

Poetic Life
First published in Great Britain in 2023 by:
DAISA PUBLISHING
An imprint of PARTNERSHIP PUBLISHING

Written By H.O.Ward
Copyright © H.O.Ward 2023

A CIP catalogue record for this book is available from the British Library.
ISBN 978-1-915200-39-6

Book Cover Design by: Partnership Publishing
Book Type Set by: Partnership Publishing

Book Published by:
PARTNERSHIP PUBLISHING
Lincolnshire
United Kingdom
www.partnershippublishing.co.uk

Printed in England.
Partnership Publishing is committed to a sustainable future for our business, our readers and our planet. This book is made from paper certified by the Forestry Stewardship Council (FSC), an organisation dedicated to promoting responsible management of forest resources.

DISCOVER AND EMBRACE THE MAGIC

Poetic Life

H.O. WARD

H . O . WARD

I was bourn in England, nineteen fifty one.
And Me and America's Rock and Roll son,
Elvis and me, we celebrate,
Every year, January eight.
He does not know, I´ll have to show him,
This publication of my poem,
Next time we´re out to lunch.
Now wait a minute, I have a hunch,
You don´t believe my claim to fame.
You think all this is just a game.
He´s still alive and going strong,
And I hope these poems last as long.
They're just to read at your leisure,
And I hope provide a moments pleasure.

CONTENTS

WAIT A MOMENT
Written February 2022
I have chosen this poem as the opener for the book
to encourage people to take just a few moments for themselves now and
again to release the stress of life.
You will be amazed just how relaxed you will feel...enjoy!

WAIT A MOMENT

Wow...stop...wait a moment,
Don't rush off...
You don't know what this is about.
What can possibly be so important
That causes you to be so hasty?
Just look at you,
You look worn out.
When was the last time you
Took a minute for yourself?
Stand still...for just a moment,
And take a deeeep breath.
(Yes - now would be a good time)
Breath innnn...and out.
Now stand here quietly
For just a moment or two.
Let the world pass you by.
Don't worry, no one is looking.
No one has even noticed you.
It's really OK to take a break,
And let the world be patient.
There you go...all done...
How hard was that...
And you're looking better now too...
Go on then...off you pop, chop-chop.

I HAVE NOT
Written April 2020

The enjoyment of walking all year round through the woods, stopping to observe its cycle of life and listen to the quiet stillness inspired this poem, and has become one of my favourites.

I HAVE NOT

I have not listened to the wind before,
Or the rustling of leaves upon the forest floor.
I have not watched the sun sparkle through the canopy,
Illuminating, as a spotlight, fresh patches of damsel buds
That open their glow of petals hue accessible to the bee.
When trees converse in unison with plants and creatures
Of another world, they pause in silence and quietly listen;
They stand in harmony and accord, all creatures of the forest.
I have not seen a timid deer, or spied at far an elusive cuckoo,
Or come across a badgers track, or witnessed squirrel in a tree.
I have not seen them, seen not one, but clearly, they have all seen me.
Within the whisper of the wind, passing through the canopy,
Disturbance of the rustling leaves scattered across the crispy floor,
Within that eerie woodland sound when the owl singularly hoots,
Your presence upon the forest floor, too all, has been announced.
But I will learn the song of wind and movement of the leaves,
And I will learn to stand so still that I may hear the silence.
I will pause in harmony with all the forest's creatures,
And I will stand in unison and learn, that which I have not.

TIME
Written December 2017
I researched and studied the mystery of the order of time,
while writing my novel Across The Parallel. This poem is a by-product
of that research...

TIME

Tis time to think of time
And in this time take the time
To contemplate of time gone by
And wonder of the time to come.
Time has come and time has gone
Yet still there's time to come.
Time flies by and there are times
When time stands still
Or time has passed you by.
Time is now and there was a time
To let the time go by
And wait until the right time,
Time and time again.
But by the time you take the time
There is not time enough.
So take the time to find the time
And spend your time
With someone that you love.

REMEMBER THE NIGHT
Written November 2002
I'm sure we can all remember those dark scary moments
from our childhood when left alone in bed...

REMEMBER THE NIGHT

He came in, silent, through the door.
I heard his footsteps across the floor.
I lay quiet still and held my breath.
The silence fills with fear and death.
Lonely in the darkest night,
Shadows in distorted light.
Listening for another sound
Only for my heart to pound.
Saliva drying from my lips,
And sweating at my fingertips,
The creaking noise upon the stair,
Oh my God, there's someone there.
Silence ringing in my ear,
I hope he doesn't know I'm here.
He's standing there outside the door,
Waiting there forever more.

ROUND THE FOUNTAIN
Written February 1992
This is probably my first worthy poem,
I wrote it while sailing round the Mediterranean Sea,
and it was selected for publication by the American Poetry Society.

ROUND THE FOUNTAIN

Upon a rippled surface
Falls a calming dance,
With arched rainbows
In cascading mist
Reflected in the glazed eyes
Of vagrants, pissed.
Polished fish spew
Silver shafts of crystal beads,
Their rhythm calm,
Yet fall chaotic.
Sparkle...Splash
To reaching hands
Requesting cash.
An endless motion
Of tranquil trance
Contained in water
From the fountain.
For these wise men
Life's a mountain.

MY LIFE

Oh my gosh, you'd never believe the life I've lead,
And I'm quite surprised that I'm not dead…already.
Yeah, I've been and gone and done most things,
And it's perhaps a good job I've not had wings,
Cos then for sure I would have killed me self.
Ya know, I never were a baby, not that I remember,
And school were just for kids, and me brother.

And me mother…well,
She would find me down the dog track,
Or pushing me barra, taking scrap,
Or down the allotment, playing cards in the shed,
Then she'd chase me home and send me to bed,
And threaten to tell me dad.
Wow, then it were trouble!

I were still a virgin till I were twelve,
When some lass lead me astray.
It were innocence really, you know how it is,
We just got carried away.
We had no kids, well, not with her,
With another lass, later on,
I had a daughter and a son.

I started work as a butcher's boy, delivering on a bike.
Then I did a window round, till winter come,
And that I didn't like.
It were freezin up the ladder and freezin on me hands,
It were just the freezin-freezin I really couldn't stand.

So I turned on all me charm and started selling cars.
I wore a suit, a fancy tie, put polish on me shoe.
It's how I met the misses, cos she thought I were a star,
Driving round the town all day lookin like who knows who.

I nearly joined the army, but I'd have had to go away
And the misses and the children, they wanted me to stay.

So I thought of them an settled down an got a proper job,
Selling on the market, to earn meself a few bob, or three!

Well that's me life of ups an downs
Without one ounce of sorrow.

We're having a party, the family and me,

Cos I'm twenty-one tomorrow!

MY LOVE
Written May 2002

I was sound asleep in my bed in Texas, America, when I suddenly woke up
and wrote this poem.

It took me approximately ten to fifteen minutes to write.

Unknowingly, and at the time I awoke, my uncle in England died.

Later that day I received a phone call to inform me of my uncle's death.

To my mind, this was a message from my uncle to his family and I posted
the poem to my aunt.

God bless and rest in peace.

MY LOVE

Think of me not far away
In quiet moments of your day
Whispers in the rustling leaves
Touching cheeks on the breeze
High among the stars each night
Feel my love burning bright
I am with you every day
Think of me not far away

I TALK TO THE WALL
Written February 2020
Many people who have read my poetry like this poem.
I wonder if it's because it plays a similar roll to a wall?

I TALK TO THE WALL

I talk to the wall
Not because I'm going crazy
Not because I'm in this cell
Not because I'm sad and lonely
Not because I'm not too well
Not because I'm getting old
Not because I have no friends
Not because I want to practice
Not because, well that depends
Not because I'm feeling angry
Not because I'm on the fence
Not because I'm all alone
Not because I make no sense
I talk to the wall
Not because I just like talking
But because
Without interruption
Without opinion
Without the murmur of a comment
The thing just stands and listens

HAIKU POETRY
Haiku Poetry Has Three Lines
They Begin With One Of Five Words
Then Seven and Finally Five

Haiku Poems are for reflection
Sit quietly and read with open mind
Contemplate the image that evokes

HAIKU POETRY

'What if', stirs the imagination
Conjures emotional aspirations deep within the soul
For that which you desire

To wander through the woodland
The Ash, Beech, Hazel, Larch, and Holly
To wander through your past

When someone is talking, listen
And you may just learn something new
To learn is to listen

THE SILLY MAGICIAN
Written December 1993
A Dutch Christmas Tradition of pass the parcel,
was the inspiration for this light-hearted poem.

THE SILLY MAGICIAN

Ladies and Gentlemen,

I'll stand not sit
And with a little bit of wit
I'll show you a magic trick.
Now, just by habit
In this box, I put a rabbit,
Or was it a hen?
I'll open it then
And let's find out.
Carefully, so it does not get out.
Sometimes I know lots of things
Sometimes I don't know how!
Now in that box I put a bird that sings.
As you can see, I could not get a cow.
Now lick your lips and count to ten,
A bird that sings is not a hen.
I wonder what happened to the rabbit,
It's such a silly habit.
I must remember, quick
And get on with the magic bit.

Now in this box
I put a rabbit
Or was it a fox?
I'll open it quickly again
As it might have eaten the hen.
Oh, look…another box,
What ever happened to the fox?
I'll not give up on this trick,
So forget the hen
Let's start again
And get on with the magic bit.

Ladies and Gentlemen,

In this little magic box
Just by habit
I put a rabbit,
A bird that sings and a chicken.
Then I did a dangerous thing!
For in this little magic box
I put a fox
And a big grizzly bear

Abracadabra

Don't lick your lips or count to ten
I don't have a habit
There is no rabbit
Or bird that sings or stupid hen.
The magic box
Has lost the fox.
I do not kid,
Let's open the lid.

Oh...the Bear!

Look, it's not there.

Take the tong of a toad
And the tail of a rat
Scorch them with fire
Add wings of a bat
Abracadabra Alakazam
Hocus Pocus Sim Sala Bim
Evil and darkness these words will inspire
These are the spells all witches desire

A WITCHES SPELL
Written December 2019
Ha Ha! Be careful if you read them aloud...it's a spell!

A WITCHES SPELL

Spit on the floor
Add the leg of a frog
Stir in Lark's vomit
And hair of a dog
Stir it thrice round
Then scratch it across
Sim Sala Bim speak the name you desire
This evil spell sets your enemy on fire

Into a clay bowl
Toss a virgin's toenail
Add feather of crow
A wishbone that's pale
Stir in some warm vampire blood
Hocus Pocus add the beak of a chicken
And slowly look deeply in the potion
The magic to freeze people in motion

Place two starling's skeleton
With the eyes of five mice
Add donkey's warm urine
Two drips added thrice
Garnish with red chicken claws
Be sure to make certain none of its yours
This is a potion to find love so they say
If sipped as a smoothie...twice a day

FEELINGS, WET

Written May 2002

This is one of my favourite poems.

To me the last line evokes emotion and stirs the senses...

FEELINGS, WET

In the cold wet and damp
Uncertain of the swirling mist
Or moments in the humid haze
A wish for cool and gentle rain
And battling through a thunderstorm
To walk upon the dew at dawn

THE VIRGIN BLANKET
Written December 2020
The fact that this winter event now happens less and less,
has inspired me to write this poem in both anticipation
and for those who have not experienced the magic...

THE VIRGIN BLANKET

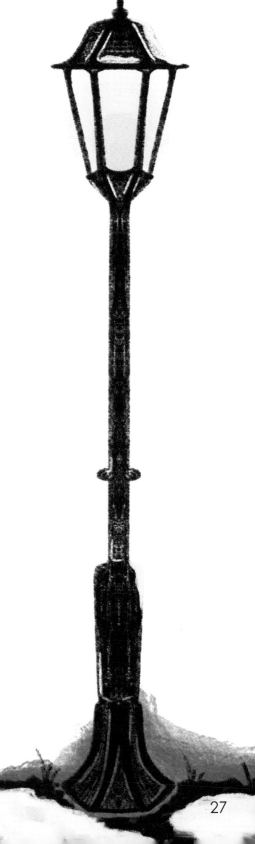

Dusk falls,
Street and field, woodland and hilltop,
Surrender to the mood of darkness.
Windowpane and streetlight illuminate,
Cascading transparent blankets of yellow hue
To settle upon the grey shades of night.
The cool air rests so still and crisp,
Absent of the weakest breeze.
Silence in the still sprawling countryside,
Stillness in the silent empty street,
Darkness whispers all around
In shadow faint and dark and deep.
Gentle delicate flakes flutter down,
Falling across the rolling hilltop,
Drifting over furrowed field,
Settling upon the manicured lawn.
Time slips by, sleepy hours pass.
Still the flakes in silent abundance fall.
Now the ground is pillow smooth,
A white wash covers every trace.
The diamond sparkle of the dawning sun
Rises slowly above cotton covered hills
Glints and glitters upon even covered rooftops.
Lonely streetlights cast their morning shadow,
Reaching long and narrow and sharp upon
The morning's white and fragile virgin blanket.

HAIKU POETRY

Remember Haiku Poetry require a pause for thought
and contemplation...

HAIKU POETRY

The writing on the wall
Each worried smile hides an anxious thought
What will the future bring?

If you could start again
And change the thing that went wrong
Would you want to try

So why do we marvel
At the beauty of our unique planet
Then go and trash it

Apply patience to your day
Allow the time to apply the magic
And see your challenge through

Along the road you travel
You have two things as your guide
Your desire and your belief

A strong wind blows freely
It shakes the branches of your mind
And brings about a change

THE EYES OF THE UNIVERSE

Be not political or judgemental,
Hold not bitterness nor revenge.
Strive to learn a humble path
And contemplate all human wrath.
Life's bitter blow or unjust wrong
Mere reflections within life's karma.
Broken tooth, nay blinded eye,
Tis better let the hurt go by.
Within the yin, there lays yang,
Within each heart a demon,
Control not your wayward brother
But reflect back all his colour.
Bring forth visions of the soul
Not drain away its beauty.
The life we share, this universe,
Its harmony is our duty.

Be not political or judgemental,
Hold no bitterness nor seek revenge.
Negativity lies both heavy and long
It drains the soul, distorts its song.
Reflect such darkness back to light
Bring forth vision to direct the right.
Within the yang, there lays yin,
Within each heart a demon,
Control not your wayward sister
But show example like no other.
Karma requires your contemplation
And echoes meaning for reflection,
Its wisdom to the future reaching
The spiritual content of its teaching.

If you believe or if you don't...
The eyes of the universe are always watching you.

CHING SHIH
Written March 2020

It was interesting to find out about Ching Shih, a woman pirate that ruled the South China Sea between 1801 and 1810.

Born as Shi Yang in 1775 she married a notorious pirate at the age of 26 and became the leader of his pirate fleet upon his death.

She operated out of Guangdong and died peacefully in Macau in 1844, at the age of 68.

There is a small temple in Macau to honour her life, which is an experience to visit.

CHING SHIH

Ching Shih, terror of the China Sea,
The most fearsome pirate in history.
Three hundred strong her Red
Flag fleet,
With forty thousand sea dogs
bowing at her feet.
British, French, and Portuguese
Wary of the China Seas.
In one attack upon the French, she,
Ching Shih,
Lead her fleet of junks to victory.
"Man the decks," she bellowed,
"To your cannons and reload.
Take one last dram of fiery grog
Before we sink this lonely frog.
Come about to starboard,
Prepare to go aboard,
Muskets to the ready boys,"
She called above the noise.
"Fire one, and fire two and fire
along the line.
This bounty rich Frenchman is
going to be mine.
Heave ho me hearties, blow the
men down,

With cutlass all ye sea dogs, let
the scallywags drown.
Take no prisoners, spare no life,"
She wants no further strife.
"We'll scuttle this old galleon,
And plunder her medallion.
Then when we're done and
finished we'll beat upon the drum,
And dance a jig and sing a song
and drink a lot more rum.
Shiver me timbers my old salts
we're three sheets to the wind.
Yo ho ho," Ching Shih calls and
holds aloft her cutlass.
"To victory my old salts, not one
of you were gutless.
Heave ho me hearties the booty
you have won,
Now steer to west my coxswain
into the setting sun."

THE LIGHTHOUSE
Written January 2019
I have experienced the importance of the lighthouse
While sailing in the Mediterranean Sea...
Having stood the test of time the advent of GPS is gradually
making these magnificent buildings redundant...
I'm sure a poem about GPS would not be so romantic...

THE LIGHTHOUSE

It is out there,
It is always out there.
Like the Puffin and the Gull,
Perched upon serrated clifftops,
Perched upon wild and windy ridges.
Nestled within the sandy dunes
With Peewits and squawking Terns,
On long, long, windswept beaches,
It is always out there.
On inaccessible headland rocks,
High upon dark and ragged cliffs,
Shared only with a gang of Gannets.
Where sea strokes the soft sand slopes
And dashes violent onto jagged rocks.
Where seabirds soar and swoop on high,
It is always out there.
Tall and silent, alone in the gales.
Resilient, majestic, alone in the storm.
Peaceful and calm, alone in the night.
A warning of peril, the lone beacon light.

THE MOMENT
Written January 2020

This poem is the result of a workshop exercise to write about a conversation between yourself and an object.

I hope you grasp the object I chose through the poem; if not I think the picture provides sufficient clues to my choice.

THE MOMENT

Yes, you might see through me,
But I see you, I see you dither,
If I, what if, maybe thoughts.
You're never sure of what you want,
Even when I show it to you, eye to eye,
You never see what I see.
There's always something, another view,
Or maybe you don't know what you want
And I'm not clever enough to know it.
Sunrise, sunset, you hide it all in shadow.
Never in the light of day do you display
Sharp and focused detail, you hide it away.
No black and white that is clear for me to see,
You surround it all with mystery.
I want to shoot…you…pause and wait.
This is not the moment, you hesitate.
Poised and ready you stare right through me,
Your heart stops beating as I shoot,
And together we capture for your memory
A moment that you'll cherish.

COFFEE BREAK
Written May 2002
Well you are about half way through the book...
Could I suggest you put the kettle on and enjoy a...

Coffee Break

COFFEE BREAK

Sitting at the table
Having coffee served by Mabel
Brings relief because you're able
With your legs under the table
To remove your horrid shoes from off your feet

The coffee with its cream
And aroma in its steam
Help relax you as you dream
For ten minutes, so supreme
Away from all the bustle of the street

Above the cups that clatter
There's the early morning chatter
Of important things that matter
While the children pitter patter
Round all the lovely people that you meet

And when the cup is empty
Of the coffee that was plenty
You begin to make your entry
With your payment complimentary
Into the days familiar jungle beat

DO I CARE?

What will the world think of me,
Do I care, am I bothered?
I've lead a life of ruffled feather,
Struggled on through stormy weather
And survived the tasks life presented,
Without much help from anyone really.
I wouldn't say my life's been dreary
But most of it seams full of chores,
With little time to sing and dance
And even less for real romance.

Do I care, am I bothered?
Well yes, I am, and no I can't be,
Otherwise it wouldn't be like this.
I thought my life would be full of bliss,
Full of laughter and happy ever after,
But that really ever happens, I guess!
I look and wonder, what a mess,
I've tried hard to do my best.
Think of others, put them first,
Just to watch the bubbles burst.

Do I care, am I bothered?
I'm not really bothered what people think,
They usually talk about things that stink,
Or stick their nose where it's not wanted
And gossip, at the wrong end of the stick.
But they also gather round, when you're sick,
Do the shopping or help with the washing.
Generally, we are all good neighbours
And we all live lives so outrageous,
Yet they're all filled with similarity.

Do I care, am I bothered?
Yes I care, and yes I'm bothered…but,
I'm not a celebrity or movie star
And my money doesn't stretch that far.
I'm not about to change the world,
And should I live for eternity,
The world will think what it wants of me.

THE FISHERMAN
Written January 2019

THE FISHERMAN

Between the reed's tall slender stems
Harsh sunlight glints in cattle tracks
And sparkles sharp among the reeds,
Where Bunting flit, from stem to stem.
Frogs eyes protrude the mirror surface.
As Boatman skim the surface tension,
Their dance reflected beneath the water.
A lark sings and chirps high on high,
Winds breeze ripples across the pond
As bright sunlight softens to shadow
And cotton clouds shimmer their reflection.
A small red speckle floats upon the still water.
It bobbles twice, and disappears.
The surface swirls, a single splash
Ripples swiftly circle across the water.
Mallards quack and scurry from the bank.
In the shallows, a crescendo of splashing.
Gone is the frog, Bunting took to their wing.
Nature fell silent throughout the excitement.
When drama passed, the Mallards swam back,
The Lark began singing, the Boatman skimming.
The Bunting returned to the reeds in the water,
The bees and butterfly now busy in the buttercups,
And the sun glistens bright on the Trout in the grass.

HAIKU POETRY

Sex Booze Rock n Roll
Are good for a while...but then
There is more to life

The order of space time
Universal consciousness determines your future is known
Before it become your history

The speaking of our words
Have effect on the people around us
Keep them thoughtful and kind

The beauty of a rainbow
A crescent hue in a darkened sky
Brings you hope not sorrow

Sitting on the park bench
Perhaps you are invisible to passers by
When thoughts are far away

If you should go there
Think of those who have gone before
As they thought of you

Today I'm concerned and wondering
What effect eight weeks sun will have
Upon the melting arctic ice

Leave me on the hilltop
In the wind and rain and snow
Let me fly my kite

In anxious moments you cry
Be still and listen to your emotions
Understand what their message says

Stand and listen in silence
Observe nature's wonderland in all its glory
Witness the winds of change

The river flows down hill
To wash away the troubles of life
Then bring a fresh tomorrow

Once they played with imagination
Today a technological influence controls their aspiration
So short is their innocence

THE TIME MACHINE
Written September 2019
The order of space-time is such
that walking east to west takes longer than walking west to east
while walking north to south takes the same time as south to north

THE TIME MACHINE

I'm standing next to a Time Machine
The strangest thing I have ever seen.
It's whirling and twirling and making a row
It sounds a little like a mooing cow.
It has flashing lights, for left and right
And spinning knobs doing their jobs.
There's something called a ponderupon,
I think it's there to sit upon
And drive the spinning thinkalater,
That works the flashing travelater.
There's something weird like a timealope,
Like looking through a kaleidoscope.
It's all controlled from the modulator
And looks a little like a perambulator.
A man is sitting on the ponderupon,
Oh my gosh…the whole things gone.

ZELDA

Written September 2021

Some time ago, the BBC showed a black and white film about a pig. The film lasted ninety minutes, without documentary or music accompaniment, in fact there was no sound track at all, just the black and white picture. However...the film was so moving it inspired me to write this poem.

Oh...have a tissue handy too, just in case!

ZELDA

The sun is high,
And blue is the sky,
Zelda lay down
in the shade of her sty.
For hour upon hour
 so still did she lay,
Her snout buried down,
covered with hay,
Lifting and flickering
with a grunting exhale
While piglets fell gently
from under her tail.
Pink and still wet
they search her small teat,
Falling and rolling
unsure on their feet.
Squeaking and crawling
and tumbling down
Zelda lay patient,
no show of a frown.
Covered in straw
with mouth unrelenting,
Two more piglets
than teats she's presenting.
Hour by hour
her litter grow stronger,
Day after day,
they're beginning to wander.

A snort and a grunt
and a push with her snout,
She keeps her young litter
controlled, just about.
Exploring the meadow,
with rolls in the mud,
Doing the things that
happy pigs should.
Her teats are now longer,
her babies well fed
She lays on her belly
when she sleep in their bed.
Then one stormy morning
with rain in the sky
Her piglets were
taken away from the sty.
It wasn't that long
that her babies were born,
Zelda was frantic and
wandered forlorn.
Grunting and snorting
she turned every stone,
Lost and bewildered
she felt so alone.
Zelda returned to her bed in the sty,
A mother forsaken she lay down to cry,
She'd lost all her babies without
a good-bye.

DUSK TO DAWN
Written October 2018

The origin of this poem derived from a writing workshop to
portray the contrast of darkness to light.

DUSK TO DAWN

Evening dusk casts it velvet shadow
That reaches out across the meadow.
In darkened woods and covered shrub
The fox will hunt to feed her cub.
The Tawny Owl in silent flight,
Catches mice throughout the night.
On the forest floor the coiled snake
Waits patiently for its pray to take.
In the darkness roam timid dear,
Each listening out with twitching ear.
And spiders spin their web of silk,
To feed upon an insects milk.
Soft light dawns to melt the shadow
Yawning gently upon the meadow.
Sparkling light on droplets of dew
That heralds in the morning new.
Scented flowers and old oak tree,
The gentle hum of the honey bee.
Buttercups catch the warm sunlight,
Each display their gold, so bright.
Sweet morning chorus from the lark,
As gentle daylight disperses dark.
So still and quiet the meadow lay,
In the early morning of the day

GOT IT...
Written January 2019
I got lost writing this one...
So good luck to you trying to read it
Let alone understand it...

GOT IT...

Wait a minute, wait a minute, wait a minute,
You can't just say something when it isn't.
You can't say what it was, if it isn't what it is,
And you can't say that it is, cos it was.

You have to say it is as it is,
Not say it as it was as it is,
Cos it's never as it is as it was,
When it was what it was as it is.

If it is what it is and not what it was,
It can't be what it is when it's not.
It's got to be what it is what it is,
Not what it is as it was.

Cos when it's what it is what it is,
It's not what it is when it's not.
It's when it's when it is what it is,
That it is as it is as it was.

Got it?

THE UNDERWORLD
Written February 2020

I like this poem,
but then we all like a bit of horror.
It has an easy readable flow that is not too scary,
even for bedtime stories.

Argh...come to me...he he heee

THE UNDERWORLD

In dark and silent alleyways
Betwixt the neon street,
Exists an evil underworld
You never want to meet.
When sun descends and shadows fall,
Trolls they stalk the darkened wall.
As the alley begins to come alive
Dogs they scarper to survive.
Hissing cats with reflecting eyes
Call to you with baby cries.
Bats through darkness swoop
and flutter,
While all along the alleys gutter
Rats they scurry to and fro,
Where you never really ought to go.
Owls they hoot in eerie chorus,
As evil starts to gently call us.
Betwixt the bins and refuse sack
Where everything looks dark
and black,

Witches hide their warts and face,
And ghouls wait in a shadowed place,
Until the magic witching hour,
And darkness fills with evil power.
When midnight strikes
And the moon is full,
The underworld is waiting,
With evil in the making.
Towards the neon flooded street
Darkness calls, inviting you
On breath that gently whispers.
Step inside, come to me,
My brothers and my sisters.

HIS LAST SHOWER
Written February 2019
Some things should never be allowed to be forgotten...
This is my understanding and interpretation of Auschwitz.

HIS LAST SHOWER

He stands naked in the shower.
His weak legs shake.
His toes grip the damp slippery floor.
His zebra skin uniquely striped,
Where sweat had run and washed it white.
His hands look oddly large at the end of his long
Thin skeletal arms. He lifted them,
Placed his palms over his sunken eyes
And gently rubbed. His fingers trembled,
Frail with swollen arthritic knuckles.
His cheek bones high, his cheeks hollow.
His teeth strong and white, loose in their socket.
His hair thick and matted, with flecks of soot.
His stomach ballooned like a pregnant wife.
His ribs protruding like prison bars.
His thoughts...
Who knows his thoughts.
Standing there like a tree in a forest,
While the shower hissed a sour taste.

SWAN AND SWALLOW
Written October 2019
Many presentations about nature these days are not complete
without the mention and reference to global warming
and pollution of our environment...so here is mine...

SWAN AND SWALLOW

Flat upon the pond's
surface like a lily leaf,
There floats a deadly
plastic bloom,
Resting still
without motion or life,
Stagnant remnants
from a commercial boom,
Poisoning the habitat,
Where swan and swallow
 would swim and skim,
Once upon a time.

Tangled amongst the
lake's tall reeds,
Windblown discarded
plastic petals gather,
Their everlasting blossom
grows forlorn,
These latent remnants
waving in the breeze,
Cluttering the habitat,
Where swan and swallow
would swim and skim,
Once upon a time.

Gathered along deserted
river banks,
Stealthily drifting
in slow flowing water,
Floats ever-growing
never popping plastic garbage,
Clear and coloured
these croutons mass,
Choking the habitat,
Where swans and swallows
would swim and skim,
Once upon a time.

When idle ponds lay
choked with plastic lily pads,
And reeds plastic blossom
swamps stagnant lakes,
Rivers float a canapé cocktail
of bottle croutons,
Take heed it is too late
when water lays polluted,
Gone is the habitat,
Where swans and swallows
did swim and skim,
Once upon a time.

HAIKU POETRY

You look out every day
All around you is just the same
You see not the changes

Please don't leave me now
You hold the strings to a puppet
Whose life will just collapse

How high the mountain stands
Bare of trees covered in cold cold snow
Tough the challenge of aspiration

Land lays soft and moist
Bright colour sits upon the artist brush
Flow the stream of life

High above the Gannets soar
At sea they hunt the silver fish
Their stomach filled with plastic

Struggling to find the words
When the time passes by so quick
Your eyes show true emotion

IT WAS JUST A THOUGHT
Written May 2002
Dementia is a sad and cruel sickness...
My poem try's to present an understanding
and was accepted by the Alzheimer Society.

IT WAS JUST A THOUGHT

For one moment I thought,
I thought,
What was my thought?
It's gone, my thought has gone.
Many of my thoughts have gone.
Once upon a time, I had many thoughts,
My thoughts would fill my head.
Now they're gone.
Well, almost gone.
Sometimes a thought would light my face,
Lift the corners of my lips,
Sparkle my eyes,
And fade.
I thought I would remember that.
Sometimes just a flash,
A thought, I thought,
But gone.

SWIMMING GOGGLES
Written April 2020

I mean...

what would you think if you saw swimming goggles in the sand?

SWIMMING GOGGLES

I went down to the sea
And strolled along the beach.
It wasn't long before I screeched,
There was something looking at me.

There protruding upwards, in the wet and soggy sand,
Facing up to look at me, a pair of swimming goggles.
I stood and stared down at them and my mind began to boggle,
Slowly I bent down to look, while reaching out my hand.

Oh my god, I jumped back up, inside were a pair of eyes.
The right eye contained bubbles, that looked like milky milk,
The rest of the swimming goggles, they were just an ilk,
That gave me a shocking surprise.

Is there someone under there?
I asked if they were all right.
I didn't want another fright,
Or just to stand and stare.

I wondered if they would answer me,
And I would help them if I could.
Then came a wave that covered up just where I was stood,
And washed away the goggles swimming back out to sea.

A NEIGHBOURLY CHAT
Written April 2020
Perhaps this poem is better understood by older readers than younger ones.

Chatting over the garden wall was the Talk-Talk chat line of the time before
mobiles and the internet.

And I recon the gossip was just as fast...
If not faster.

A NEIGHBOURLY CHAT

I saw Betty with her headscarf on,
Her head bobbling along the top of
the wall,
On her way down the garden
towards the bin.
Picking up my cuppa, I quickly
nipped outside
And took a sip of tea.
"Morning Betty," says I.
"How's Bert?" I asked, enquiring.
"Give us a fag, will ya Sheil …
Oh, he's alright, doctor says it's
just a cold."
"Well," says I,
"You'd think he were dying yesterday."
"I thought so too," says she.
"He's up there now, right as nine
pence, reading paper."
"Bring me a cuppa, will ya,"
shouts Bert.
"I'll bring you something,"
says Betty.
"Oh Betty...Men," says I.
"Their enough to drive you crazy."
"I'll tell you what," says she,

"If I'm not blinking careful, he'll be
the death of me."
"Don't say that, Betty," says I.
"He's a good bloke for you really."
"Hmm, you think so do you?
Well I'll send him round, see what
you think then,
And I'll ask you again tomorrow.
Then I'll see what you say." Says she.
"Are you there, Betty?" says Bert,
Shouting loudly from his sick bed.
"Just listen to him,
I'll have to go," says Betty,
"His tea has probably gone cold.
Thanks for the fag."
"Oh, that's alright," says I, "I think
my tea's cold too."

HOME LATE
Written December 2002
You can just imagine the trouble you would be in coming home late
after a night out with the boys.

I know...I've been there!

HOME LATE

Look at the time it's getting late,
Staying out of bed to wait
To listen to the usual excuses,
I sometimes wonder what the use is!

Oh, I've heard it all before
And the creeping through the door.
I bet there's someone else involved,
I'll get this little lot resolved.

Another row,
I feel it brewing.

But wait...
What have I been doing?

STREET SCENE
Written February 2020

Unfortunately this street scene occurs
all too frequently these days.

I wrote the poem in the hope that
people will stop and pause and reflect
on the direction of society.

STREET SCENE

Pitter-Patter, Clip-Clop,
Not many people stop.
Clip-Clop, Pitter-Patter,
Does it really matter?
I guess not.
They have their world,
I have mine,
Never will the two entwine.
They have their life,
I have mine,
And I guess that's also fine.
But somewhere in the middle
There's a sort of kind of muddle
That draws an invisible line.
Their side is theirs,
My side is mine,
That's played out every time.

They look down at me,
And I look up at them,
Because I'm usually sitting down,
But that's not what's important.
We each have our face,
We each have our space,
And sometimes a little respect.
I don't want their life,
They certainly don't want my life,
I can tell that every time.
But once in a while
We each give a smile
And share a few words with each
other.
It doesn't last long,
And nothing goes wrong,
But one is grateful for t'other.

THE EMPTINESS OF LIFE
Written 20 November 2020

THE EMPTINESS
OF LIFE

I sit woefully upon my bed,

Clasping my hands upon my lap,

Twiddling and twisting my dry worn fingers.

Grey muted light filters through my only window,

And smudges upon the four bare walls that surround me.

A single closed door, occupies the wall opposite the window.

I can hear movement and sounds beyond my walls,

But no one comes.

No one visits.

I sit here for hours,

Watching faint bland and ghostly shadows move around my walls.

Entering, uninvited through my window.

My only visitors.

Though none, not one, stops to say hello.

How long the days.

How long the nights.

How long this emptiness of life.

I hear my name rattle the windowpane.

Masked faces appear like puppets,

Their muffled voices murmuring and giggling beyond the glass.

There is no pause to listen to my cry.

Then they are gone,

And I return to the emptiness of life.

AN ELEGANT ELOQUENT ELEPHANT
Written April 2020
I hope you enjoyed some of the poems
and
like the elephant, will remember others.

Thank you for reading.

AN ELEGANT
ELOQUENT ELEPHANT

An elegant eloquent elephant, that cannot be,
There's something wrong, there has to be.
Elegant, as an adjective, means to be
Graceful and stylish in appearance or manner.
And eloquent, also an adjective, means to be fluent
Or persuasive, clearly expressive or indicative.
Where elephant, as a noun, is, as we all know,
A very large, grey coloured, plant-eating animal,
With large ears, a prehensile trunk, and long tusks.
So...
If elegant is to be graceful,
And persuasive speaking is eloquent
Then the graceful appearance
Of a very large persuasive elephant
Is good enough for me.

BOOKS BY
H.O.WARD

Released in 2021
This daring novel tells the story of George, a
Lancaster Bomber Pilot, who crosses the parallels
of life, and experiences the wisdom of the universe,
the mystery of space-time consciousness, and the
fraught history of his past...

But what lies ahead in the enigma of his future.

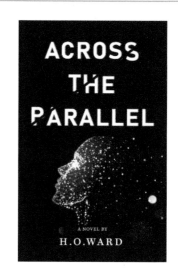

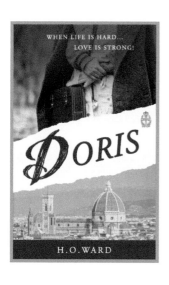

Released in 2020
This emotional roller coaster of a novel tells the
story of Dorothy, a young nurse who experiences
the drama of war, romance in Florence, and
homelessness in London.

You meet Dorothy as a homeless vagabond called
Doris. This moving story then takes you back to
explain how she became homeless.

Venice Lagoon
Coming Soon

A futuristic story of drama and intrigue. A story of love and danger.
A frightful story about the relationship between humans and robots.
A story best not told.